GOD'S
SUFFERING
SERVANT

THE STORY BIBLE SERIES

1. *God's Family* tells the story of creation, God's promises to Abraham's family, and the adventures of Joseph.

2. *God Rescues His People* tells about Israel's escape from Egypt, Moses and the Ten Commandments, and the wandering in the wilderness.

3. *God Gives the Land* tells the story of Joshua, the adventures of the judges, and the story of Ruth.

4. *God's Chosen King* tells about Samuel, Saul, and David, God's promises to David's family, and the Psalms.

5. *God's Wisdom and Power* tells about the glorious reign of Solomon, the wonderful works of Elijah and Elisha, and the Proverbs and the Song of Songs.

6. *God's Justice* tells the story of the prophets Amos, Hosea, Isaiah, and Jeremiah and their messages of God's judgment and mercy.

7. *God Comforts His People* tells about God's people in exile, their return to the land, and the adventures of Esther and Daniel.

8. *God Sends His Son* tells about God sending Jesus to set up his kingdom.

9. *God's Suffering Servant* tells about the last week of Jesus' life, his suffering, death, and resurrection.

   Book 10 will complete the retelling of the New Testament.

Story Bible Series, Book 9

GOD'S SUFFERING SERVANT

Stories of God and His People from Matthew, Mark, Luke, and John

Retold by Eve B. MacMaster
Illustrated by James Converse

HERALD PRESS
Scottdale, Pennsylvania
Kitchener, Ontario
1987

Library of Congress Cataloging-in-Publication Data

MacMaster, Eve, 1942-
  God's suffering servant.

  (Story Bible series ; bk. 9)
  Summary: A retelling of the New Testament passages
describing the events of the last week of Jesus' life
from His entry into Jerusalem until the Resurrection.
    1. Jesus Christ—Passion—Juvenile literature.
2. Jesus Christ—Resurrection—Juvenile literature.
3. Jesus Christ—Ascension—Juvenile literature.
4. Bible stories, English—N.T.   Gospels. [1. Jesus
Christ. 2. Bible stories—N.T.] I. Converse, James, ill.
II. Title. III. Series.
BT431.M27 1987   226'.09505   86-19526
ISBN 0-8361-3422-2 (pbk.)

GOD'S SUFFERING SERVANT
Copyright © 1987 by Herald Press, Scottdale, Pa. 15683
  Published simultaneously in Canada by Herald Press,
  Kitchener, Ont. N2G 4M5. All rights reserved.
Library of Congress Catalog Card Number: 86-19526
International Standard Book Number: 0-8361-3422-2
Printed in the United States of America

92   91   90   89   88   87   10   9   8   7   6   5   4   3   2   1

The Story of This Book

Several years ago I was looking for a Bible story book to read to my children. I wanted one that was complete, without tacked-on morals or a denominational interpretation. I wanted one that was faithful to the Bible and fun to read. I couldn't find what I was looking for.

With the encouragement of my husband, Richard MacMaster, I approached Herald Press with the idea of the series: a retelling of the whole Bible with nothing added and nothing subtracted, just following the story line through the Old and New Testaments.

The people at Herald Press were agreeable and enthusiastic and gave much valuable advice, especially general book editor Paul M. Schrock.

At his suggestion, I asked some academic and professional people in our community to check the stories for style and accuracy. Members of the advisory committee, who have kindly volunteered their time, include Bible professors George R. Brunk III, Ronald D. Guengerich, G. Irvin Lehman, and Kenneth Seitz; and childhood curriculum and librarian specialists Elsie E. Lehman and A. Arlene Bumbaugh.

I hope this series will lead its readers to the original, for no retelling is a substitute for the Bible itself. The Bible is actually a collection of books written over a long period of time in a variety of forms. It has been translated and retold in every generation because people everywhere want to know what God is like.

The main character in every story is God. The plot of every story is God's activity among his people: creating, saving, fighting, reigning, and doing works of wisdom and power, justice and mercy.

The first book in the series is *God's Family*. It tells stories about God the Creator.

The second book is *God Rescues His People*. It tells stories about God the Savior.

The third book is *God Gives the Land*. It tells stories about God the warrior.

The fourth book, *God's Chosen King*, tells stories about God the true King.

The fifth book, *God's Wisdom and Power*, tells stories about God, the source of wisdom and power.

The sixth book, *God's Justice*, tells stories about God the righteous Judge.

The seventh book, *God Comforts His People*, tells stories about God's comforting mercy and promises.

The eighth book, *God Sends His Son*, tells stories about how Jesus came into the world, teaching and working miracles.

This book, *God's Suffering Servant*, tells about Jesus' last days in Jerusalem, his arrest, trial, crucifixion, death and burial, and the wonderful story of his resurrection.

This volume is dedicated to the glory of Jesus Christ, whose life, death, and resurrection have made all the difference.

—Eve B. MacMaster
Bluffton, Ohio
September 8, 1986

Contents

God Shows His Glory

Map

The Author

God Visits
His People

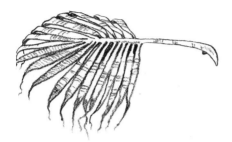

1

"Your King Is Coming!"

Matthew 21; Mark 11; Luke 19; John 12

THE people of Jerusalem were excited. The rabbi Jesus was on his way from Galilee. He was coming to Jerusalem for the great feast of Passover, and a crowd of people was following him.

Some people wanted to make Jesus king. They were saying that he was God's anointed ruler, the Messiah they were waiting for.

This teacher Jesus was certainly anointed by God. He had shown the power of God by healing the sick and driving out demons. He had opened the eyes of the blind and the ears of the deaf. He had even raised a man from the dead.

Perhaps, said the people, Jesus was the one the ancient prophets had spoken about. Perhaps he was the leader who would save them from their enemies. Perhaps he would drive out the Romans and set up the kingdom of God. Perhaps he would be a great warrior, like the ancient king, David.

While the people were talking, Jesus and his disciples arrived at the outskirts of the towns of Bethphage and Bethany. They were standing at the foot of the Mount of Olives, just outside Jerusalem.

Jesus sent two of his disciples ahead.

"Go into the village you see over there," he told them. "When you enter, you'll find a young donkey tied up. It will be one which nobody has ever ridden. Untie it and bring it here. If anyone asks you why you're taking it, just say, 'The teacher needs it and will send it right back.' "

The disciples went to the village and found everything just as Jesus said. The donkey was tied next to a doorway in the open street.

As they were untying it, some of the men who were standing there asked, "What are you doing? Why are you untying that colt?"

The two disciples answered as Jesus had told them, and then they took the donkey back to him. Some of his other followers spread their coats on the donkey's back, and Jesus got up on it and rode it.

The words of the ancient prophets came true in

the life of Jesus. This action fulfilled what the prophet Zechariah said:

> "Don't be afraid, daughter Zion.
>   Look! Your king is coming to you!
> "He is humble and riding on a donkey,
>   on a colt, the foal of a donkey."

Jesus was coming to Zion (a nickname for the city of Jerusalem), entering the city as a king. But he wasn't the kind of king the people were expecting.

Only later did his followers and the people of Jerusalem understand why Jesus came as a humble servant. Only later did they understand why he suffered, and who he really was.

As Jesus rode into the city, many people spread their coats on the road in front of him. Others spread branches they had cut from palm trees.

When he reached the place where the road came down from the Mount of Olives, the crowd of his followers burst into song. They were so full of joy, they sang a loud song of praise to God.

"Long live the king!" shouted the people who walked in front of him.

"Hosanna!" cried the people walking behind him.

"God save him!" they all shouted. "God bless the coming kingdom of our ancestor, David! Hosanna! Glory to God in the highest heaven!"

Some religious leaders from Jerusalem were in the crowd watching, and when they heard these shouts, they were annoyed.

"Teacher," they called to Jesus. "Tell your followers to be quiet!"

"I tell you the truth," answered Jesus. "If my disciples keep quiet, the stones will shout!"

As he came near to the city, Jesus looked at it and cried. "O Jerusalem!" he said. "If only you understood the message of peace! But it's hidden from your eyes. The time is coming when enemies will surround this city, and your people will suffer—all because you didn't recognize the time when God himself visited you!"

2

A House of Prayer for All Nations

Matthew 21; Mark 11; Luke 17, 19; John 2

JESUS and his disciples spent the night in the village of Bethany. The next morning they returned to Jerusalem. On the way into the city Jesus felt hungry. He noticed a fig tree in the distance and walked over to see if it had any fruit. He found nothing but leaves on it, for figs weren't in season yet.

"May no one ever eat any fruit of yours again!" he said to the tree. Then he went into the city with his disciples.

As they entered Jerusalem, they saw the splen-

did temple of God rising high above all the other buildings. As they climbed the hill to the temple, they smelled the smoke that curled up from the altar where the priests were offering sacrifices. Sacrifices were an important part of the Jewish religion. Because God was so holy, the people could come to him only after offering a sacrifice.

Jesus and his disciples went into the outer courtyard of the temple, the Court of the Nations. People from all nations were allowed to come here and pray. But only Jews were allowed to enter the inner courtyard and offer sacrifices.

When Jesus arrived at the Courtyard of the Nations, he found men selling live cattle, sheep, and pigeons for sacrifices. Other men were sitting at tables, exchanging Roman coins for special temple coins.

Jesus drove the whole pack of them out of the temple area, along with their cattle and sheep. He overturned the tables of the money changers, spilling their coins. He wouldn't let anyone carry merchandise through the courtyard.

"Get them out of here!" he shouted to the pigeon sellers as he knocked down their seats. "Stop turning my Father's place into a marketplace!"

Then he said to the people who were watching, "The Scripture says:

> 'My house will be called
>   a house of prayer for all nations.
> 'But you have made it
>   a hideout for robbers!' "

The temple authorities came to Jesus and demanded an explanation. "What sign can you show us that you have the right to do this?" they asked.

Jesus answered, "Pull down this temple, and in three days I will raise it up."

"What?" they said. "It has taken forty-six years to build this temple! How could you put it up again in three days?"

He was talking about the temple of his body, but even his disciples didn't understand until later.

Jesus stayed in the temple area the rest of that day. When the blind and crippled people heard that he was there, they came to him, and he healed them.

The chief priests and religious teachers were angry when they found out what Jesus was doing. And when they heard little children in the temple area shouting, "Hosanna! Son of David!" they were furious.

"Do you hear what those children are saying?" they asked him.

"Certainly," he answered. "Haven't you read this Scripture:

'Out of the mouths of little children and tiny babies
God has caused his praises to be sung!' "

Early the next morning, as Jesus and his disciples were walking along the road to Jerusalem, they saw the fig tree again. Its leaves were dried up.

"Look, Teacher!" said Peter. He remembered what Jesus had said the day before. "The fig tree you cursed is withered!"

Jesus answered, "Have faith in God. Believe me. If you had enough faith, you could do the same thing!"

3

Jesus Teaches in the Temple

Matthew 21—22; Mark 11—12; Luke 14, 20

WHO gave you the right to do these things?"

The chief priests, scribes, and elders were questioning Jesus. These religious leaders didn't like the way the crowds were following him. They didn't like the way he was healing and teaching the people at the temple.

"Tell us," they demanded. "Who gave you the right to act this way?"

Jesus answered, "First let me ask you a question. If you give me an answer, I'll tell you who gave me the right to do these things. Now tell me, where did John's right to baptize come from? Was it from heaven or earth? From God or man? Answer me!"

They began to argue among themselves about John the Baptist.

"What should we say?"

"If we answer, 'From God,' he'll ask us why we didn't believe in John."

"But if we answer, 'From man,' the people will stone us. They're convinced that John was a prophet."

Finally they answered, "We don't know."

"Then," said Jesus, "I won't tell you who gave me the right to do these things."

While the religious leaders were still listening, Jesus told some parables. He often taught by telling these simple stories, to make people think about the kingdom of God.

"Listen!" he said. "Once there was a man who had two sons. He said to the first one, 'Son, go and work in the vineyard today.'

" 'Yes, sir,' he answered. But he didn't go.

"Then the father went to the second son and gave him the same order.

" 'I won't go,' the second son answered. But later he changed his mind and went.

"Now tell me," said Jesus. "Which of the two sons did what the father wanted?"

"The one who went to the vineyard," they answered.

"I tell you the truth," said Jesus. "Tax collectors and prostitutes are on the way to the kingdom of God ahead of you religious leaders! For John the Baptist showed you the right thing to do, but you didn't believe in him. Sinners like tax collectors and prostitutes believed in him, but even after you saw that, you didn't change your minds and believe in him."

Then Jesus told another parable.

"There was once a landowner who planted a vineyard. He built a wall around it and dug a hole for a winepress, so he could make wine from the grapes that would grow on the vines. He built a watchtower to guard his vineyard. Then he rented it to some tenant farmers and went to another country.

"When the harvest season came near and it was time to pick the grapes, the landowner sent his servants to the farmers to collect his share of the harvest. But they grabbed his servants and beat one, killed another, and threw stones at a third.

"Then the man sent other servants, more than before. But the farmers treated them the same way.

"Finally, the owner of the vineyard said to himself, 'I'll send them my own beloved son. Surely, they'll respect my son!'

"But when the farmers saw the son, they said to each other, 'This is the son and heir! Come on, let's kill him and take the property for ourselves!'

"They grabbed him and threw him out of the vineyard and killed him.

"Well, now," said Jesus. "When the owner of the vineyard comes, what do you think he'll do to those farmers?"

They answered, "He'll certainly put those wicked men to death and give the vineyard to someone else—to someone who will give him fruit!"

Jesus said, "Believe me, the kingdom of God will be given to someone else, to people who will produce fruit for the kingdom. This is the meaning of the Scripture:

'The stone which the builders rejected
    has turned out to be the cornerstone.
'This is the Lord's doing,
    and it is wonderful to see!'

"Everyone who trips over that stone will be smashed to pieces," he said. "Everyone it falls on will be crushed."

The chief priests and the scribes and the elders knew that Jesus was talking about them. He was saying that they had been given a chance to produce fruit, but had failed, like the fig tree that Jesus had withered. They knew he was comparing them to the wicked farmers, and they were furious.

They wanted to arrest Jesus immediately, but they were afraid of the people, for the people were convinced that Jesus was a prophet.

While he was teaching in the temple, Jesus told another parable about God giving the kingdom to someone else.

"Listen," he said. "The kingdom of God is like this. A king was celebrating his son's wedding. When the time came for the wedding feast, the king sent his servants to remind the guests who had been invited. But they refused to come.

"He did the same thing a second time, sending more servants. He told the servants, 'Tell the guests that I've prepared everything. The bulls and cattle have all been butchered, and everything is ready for the feast. Tell them to come to the party!'

"But they paid no attention. Instead, they went about their business as usual. One went to a farm he owned, and another went to his shop. The rest of them grabbed the king's servants and beat them and killed them.

"The king was so angry, he sent his soldiers to destroy the murderers and burn down their city. Then he said to his servants, 'The wedding feast is ready, but the people I invited first have turned out to be worthless. Now go out to the highway and invite anyone you can find.'

"They went out to the highway and gathered everyone they could find, both good and bad, so the wedding hall was filled with guests.

"When the king came in to greet the guests, he found a man who wasn't dressed for a wedding. 'My friend,' he said, 'how did you get in here without wedding clothes?'

"The man had no answer, so the king ordered his servants, 'Tie him up hand and foot, and throw him outside into the darkness, where he'll cry and grind his teeth!'

"You see," said Jesus, as he finished the story, "many are called, but few are chosen."

Jesus Answers His Enemies

Matthew 21—22; Mark 12; Luke 20

JESUS' enemies were trying to find a way to trap him. They wanted to trick him into saying something they could use against him.

These enemies were the religious leaders, and they were divided into groups that argued among themselves. But they went to Jesus together, for they hated him more than they hated each other.

The Pharisees, who followed strict rules and despised the Romans, joined with the Herodians, who cooperated with the Roman government. They agreed to pretend to be sincerely interested in doing God's will, so they could trap Jesus.

"Teacher," they said to him, "we know you're an honest man. You teach the way of God sincerely. You're not afraid of anyone, and you're not impressed with anyone, either. Now tell us, what do you think? Is it right for us to pay taxes to the Roman emperor or not?"

Jesus knew what they were up to. If he said it wasn't right to pay taxes, they would accuse him of being a traitor to the Roman government. If he said it was right to pay taxes, they would say he was a traitor to God. They would use whatever he said against him.

This tax had to be paid with a silver coin that was engraved with the image of Emperor Tiberius Caesar. The writing around Caesar's picture said he was the son of the god Augustus.

The Pharisees wouldn't even carry these coins, for it was wicked to call anyone God except the Lord.

"You hypocrites!" said Jesus. "You fakes! Why are you putting me to this test?" Then he said, "Give me a silver coin and let me look at it."

They handed him a denarius, the coin with the image of Caesar.

"Whose image is this?" he asked. "Whose name is written here?"

"Caesar's," they answered.

"Well, then," he answered, "pay to Caesar what belongs to Caesar, and to God what belongs to God!"

Jesus' answer amazed his enemies. Men and women are made "in the image of God," just as the coin was stamped with a portrait of Tiberius Caesar. The Pharisees and the Herodians couldn't find anything in Jesus' answer to use against him.

Later that day another group of religious leaders came to Jesus with another trick question. These were the Sadducees, the rich land-owners and priests who controlled the ruling council of the Jews.

The Sadducees disagreed with the Pharisees about many things. The Pharisees said that the dead would be raised to life at the end of time. The Sadducees didn't believe in this resurrection.

They decided to ask Jesus a question about the resurrection to make him and the Pharisees look foolish.

"Teacher," they said, "Moses taught that if a man dies without leaving children, his brother should marry the widow. Then they can have children to be counted as the dead man's descendants. Well, now, we have a difficult case for you.

"There were seven brothers, and the first one married and died without leaving any children. His brother married the widow. The third brother did the same thing, and so did the fourth. All seven of them married her, and all seven of them died without leaving any children. Last of all, the woman herself died.

"Now tell us. On the day of resurrection, whose wife will she be? She was married to all seven."

Jesus knew they were trying to trap him. "You're completely wrong!" he said. "You're ignorant of the Scriptures and you're ignorant of the power of God!

"When people rise from the dead," he explained, "they don't marry. They're like the angels in heaven. As for the resurrection of the dead—which you refuse to believe in—haven't you read the story of Moses and the burning bush? God said to Moses, 'I am the God of Abraham and the God of Isaac, and the God of Jacob.' He's the God of the living, not the dead. He knows they're still alive!"

When the people heard Jesus' answer, they admired him for his teaching. They realized that God's rule is greater than the Romans or any human government. They saw that God's rule is even greater than death.

After this no one dared to ask Jesus any more questions.

5

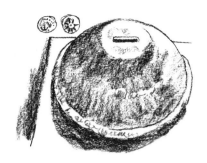

"Woe to the Pharisees!"

Matthew 23; Mark 12; Luke 11, 20—21

WATCH out!" Jesus warned his disciples. "Be on your guard against certain scribes and Pharisees. They're the official teachers of the Scriptures, so you must do what they teach. But don't copy their behavior. They don't all practice what they preach."

The Pharisees were the strictest of all the Jewish religious leaders. Some of them truly loved God and tried to please him. But others cared more about themselves than about God.

Jesus was angry with these Pharisees for confusing the common people. "Everything they do is for show," he said. "They love to wear religious robes, so everyone can see how spiritual they are. They like the best seats in the synagogues and the best places at banquets. They enjoy having people notice them and look up to them. They want to be called by titles like Rabbi.

"But these men steal the property of the poor. Then they try to prove that God is with them by saying long prayers in public.

"Don't be like them. Don't let anyone call you Rabbi, for you have only one teacher, and you're all brothers. Don't call anyone on earth Father, for you have only one Father, and he is in heaven. Don't call anyone Leader, for you have only one leader, and he is the Messiah.

"Remember, the greatest person among you isn't the one who acts like the Pharisees. Instead, it's the one who serves the others. Whoever tries to be great will be humbled, and whoever is humble will be lifted up."

Then Jesus said, "How terrible it will be for the scribes and Pharisees! Woe to you Pharisees! You hypocrites! You fakes! You shut the door of the kingdom of God in people's faces. You won't go in yourselves, but you won't let anyone else in either. You make God's teaching seem repulsive!

"You travel over land and sea to win one person to your side, and when you do, he's twice as bad as you are!

"You carefully measure your belongings—even

your garden herbs—to give God exactly one tenth of what you have. And all the time, you completely ignore God's important teachings about justice and mercy!

"You blind guides! You strain a fly out of your drink, and then you swallow a camel!

"You're like whitewashed tombs. They look fine on the outside, but inside they're full of dead men's bones and all kinds of filth and decay. In

the same way, you look nice from the outside, but inside you're full of lies and sin!

"You snakes! You build tombs for the prophets, and monuments to the holy men your ancestors killed. Then you go on persecuting the messengers that God sends to you. Well, go on! Finish the work your ancestors started!"

Jesus was saying these things while he was sitting in the temple area. He was in a position where he could see people putting money into the offering box in the temple treasury. He watched many rich men dropping a lot of money into the box. Then he noticed a poor widow putting in two tiny copper coins.

"Believe me," he said, calling his disciples to see. "This poor widow has given more than all the others! They have more than they need, and they gave from what they had left over. But she has less than she needs. She gave everything she has to live on."

6

The Fall of Jerusalem

Matthew 23—24; Mark 13; Luke 17, 19, 21

O Jerusalem!" cried Jesus. "Jerusalem! The city that murders the prophets and stones the messengers that God sends to you! How many times I have wanted to put my arms around all your people, as a hen gathers her chicks under her wings! But you wouldn't let me."

Later, as Jesus was leaving the temple area, one of the disciples said, "Look, what mighty blocks of stone! What magnificent buildings!

Jesus answered, "You see these great temple buildings? Not a block of stone will be left standing on top of another. Everything will be torn down. The temple will be destroyed. Everything will be left empty and forsaken."

As Jesus was sitting on the Mount of Olives, across the Kidron Valley from Jerusalem, Peter, James, John, and Andrew came to him.

"Tell us," said the disciples, "when is this going to happen? What sign will there be?"

Jesus answered, "Nobody knows when this will happen, but you must be prepared."

Then he told them what it was going to be like in the days before Jerusalem was destroyed. "You'll hear lies. People will use my name, trying to trick you. You'll hear about wars. Don't be upset. These things must happen, but they don't mean the end is near.

"There will be wars and earthquakes and famines and terrifying signs from heaven. These things are just the beginning of the labor pains as the new age is being born.

"Watch out! Before these things happen, you'll be arrested and tortured. They'll drag you into courts and beat you in synagogues. You'll be brought in front of kings and governors because of me. That will be your chance to tell them of your faith in me.

"When they arrest you and take you away, don't worry about what to say. Don't prepare speeches to defend yourself. But when the time comes, use the words that I will give you through the Holy Spirit.

"In those days, there will be so much evil that members of the same family will turn against each other. Some of you will even be killed. But everyone who stands firm to the end will be saved. Before the end, the good news of the kingdom of God must be preached to all nations.

"Do you remember the story in the book of Daniel about the Abomination of Desolation?" he asked. "Well, when you see that awful idol standing in the holy place inside the temple, you'll know that it's time for the people of Judea to run to the hills. Terrible suffering will come to Jerusalem. False messiahs and false prophets will try to trick God's people. Watch out!

"After this time of trouble, the sun will be darkened, and the moon won't give its light. The stars will fall from the sky, and the mighty ones of heaven will be shaken.

"Then the Son of Man will appear. All the people on earth will see him coming in clouds with great power and glory. With the sound of a loud trumpet, he will send angels to gather together his chosen ones from all over the world.

"When will this happen? Learn a lesson from the fig tree. When you see its branches turn green and its leaves come out, you know summer is near.

"In the same way, when you see these things happening, you'll know that the time is near. I tell you the truth. All this will happen before the people now living have died.

"Heaven and earth will pass away, but my words will never pass away.

"No one knows the day or the hour when these things will happen—not the angels in heaven, not even the Son—only the Father knows."

7

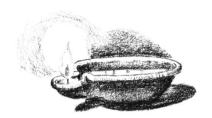

Be Prepared!

Matthew 24—25; Mark 13; Luke 12, 17, 19, 21

BE PREPARED!" Jesus warned his disciples. "The kingdom of God doesn't come the way you expect.

"The coming of the Son of Man will be like the time of Noah. In the days before the flood, people were living their lives as usual, all the way up to the very day that Noah went into the ark. They didn't understand what was going on until the water came and washed them all away. That's what it's going to be like when the Son of Man appears.

"Stay awake. Watch out! You don't know the time your master is coming. The Son of Man will come suddenly, without warning, like a thief in the night. It might be evening or midnight or daybreak. I warn you, watch out!"

Then Jesus told his disciples a parable about the coming of the Son of Man.

"Once there were ten bridesmaids. They went out to meet the bridegroom, who was on his way to the bride's house for the wedding party. They took their oil lamps to light the way to the house.

"Five of the girls were foolish, and five of them were wise. The foolish ones took their lamps but forgot to take extra oil. The wise bridesmaids remembered to take extra oil.

"The bridegroom was late, so the bridesmaids became sleepy. In the middle of the night, as they were lying down, they heard someone shouting, 'The bridegroom is here! Come and meet him!'

"The ten bridesmaids woke up and lit their lamps. The foolish girls said to the wise ones, 'Give us some of your oil, for our lamps are going out.'

"The wise girls answered, 'There might not be enough for all of us. You go to the market and buy some for yourselves.'

"While the five foolish girls were out buying oil, the bridegroom arrived. The five wise girls went in to the wedding with him, and the door was shut.

"Later the other girls arrived. 'Lord! Lord!'

they cried. 'Open the door and let us in!'

"But he answered, 'I tell you the truth, I don't know you.'

"Watch out!" Jesus warned. "Be prepared. You don't know the day or the hour when the Son of Man will come!"

Later, the disciples understood that he was talking about himself.

Then he told them another parable. This story was about the Last Judgment, at the end of time.

"When the Son of Man comes," he said, "in his glory with all the angels, he'll sit on his magnificent throne. All the nations will be gathered in front of him, and he'll sort the people out. He'll divide them as a shepherd divides the sheep and the goats. He'll put the sheep on his right side and the goats on his left.

"Then the King will say to the ones on his right, 'Come, you blessed ones who belong to my Father! Come and take your inheritance. The kingdom has been prepared for you since the foundation of the earth.

" 'For I was hungry, and you gave me food. I was thirsty, and you gave me a drink. I was homeless, and you took me in. I was naked, and you clothed me. I was sick, and you visited me. I was in prison, and you came to me.'

"Then the righteous ones will answer, 'Lord, when did we see you hungry and feed you? Or see you thirsty and give you a drink? When did we see you homeless and take you in? Or naked, and clothe you? When did we see you sick or in prison and visit you?'

"The King will answer, 'I tell you the truth, whenever you did these things for one of the poorest of my brothers, you did them for me.'

"Then he will say to the ones on his left side, 'Go away, you who are cursed! Go to the eternal fire, prepared for the devil and his angels.

" 'For I was hungry, and you didn't feed me. I was thirsty, and you didn't give me a drink. I was homeless, and you didn't take me in, naked, and you didn't clothe me, sick and in prison, and you didn't visit me.'

"Then they will say to him, 'Lord, when did we

see you hungry or thirsty, or homeless or naked, or sick or in prison, and fail to help you?'

"The King will say to them, 'I tell you truly, whenever you failed to do these things for one of the poorest of my brothers, you failed to do them for me.'

"Then they will go away to eternal punishment, while the righteous will enter into eternal life."

Jesus' Farewell to His Friends

Jesus Is Anointed
and Betrayed

Matthew 26; Mark 14; Luke 22; John 12—13

JESUS knew that his enemies were plotting against him. "You realize," he said to his disciples, "in two days it will be Passover. Then the Son of Man will be handed over to be crucified."

Every morning during that Passover week, the people gathered around Jesus in the courtyard of the temple. They listened carefully to his teaching, and many of them believed in him.

Every morning the chief priests, the scribes, and the elders gathered together in the courtyard of the high priest's palace to make plans for getting rid of Jesus. They wanted to have him arrested and condemned to death, but they wanted to do it secretly, because they were afraid of the people.

"It must not be during the Passover festival," they said to each other. "The people might riot."

If there were a riot, these religious leaders would be in danger. The Romans might come and take away their power.

The chief priests, scribes, and elders kept on plotting. But everything happened that week just as Jesus said it would, not as the leaders plotted.

One evening Jesus was in Bethany. Martha served a dinner in Jesus' honor. Lazarus and Mary were also there. Mary took some expensive perfume and poured it on Jesus' feet. Then she wiped his feet with her hair.

When the disciples saw what was going on, they were annoyed. "Why this waste?" they complained.

"Why wasn't the perfume sold?" asked Judas Iscariot. "It's worth three hundred pieces of silver. The money could have been given to the poor."

Judas didn't say this because he cared about the poor, but because he was a thief. He was in charge of the money bag for all the disciples, and he often helped himself to it.

"Leave this woman alone!" Jesus said. "Why are you scolding her? She has done a beautiful thing for me."

Then he explained to them, "You'll always have poor people among you. But you won't always have me with you. By pouring this ointment on my body, she was preparing it for burial. Wherever in the whole world the good news of the kingdom is preached, what this woman did will also be told, and she will be remembered."

After Jesus said this, Judas Iscariot left the house and went to the chief priests.

"What would you give me if I handed Jesus over to you?" he asked them.

They were delighted to hear what Judas wanted, and they promised to pay him thirty pieces of silver. That was the usual price for selling a slave.

From that time on, Judas was looking for a chance to betray Jesus.

9

Jesus Washes His Disciples' Feet

Matthew 26; Mark 14; Luke 22; John 13

PASSOVER was the most important of all the Jewish festivals. It was celebrated every year to remind the Jews how the Lord their God had saved them from slavery in Egypt. At Passover time, they met together in family groups and ate a special meal of roast lamb, bread baked without yeast, and bitter herbs.

The Passover lamb had to be young and perfect. When it was killed, its bones weren't broken. The ancient Israelites, the ancestors of the Jews, had smeared the blood of the Passover lamb over the tops and sides of the door frames of their houses in Egypt, so that the Angel of Death would pass over them. Each Passover since that time, the Jews remembered that the blood of the lamb was the price of their freedom.

This year Jesus was going to give Passover new meaning.

When the day came for the special meal to be eaten, he said to Peter and John, "Go and make the preparations for us to eat the Passover."

"Where do you want us to prepare it?" they asked.

"Go into the city," he said. "As soon as you enter, you'll meet a man carrying a jug of water. Follow him, and when he enters a house, tell the owner, 'The Teacher wants to know which room he can eat the Passover supper in with his disciples.' He'll show you a large upstairs room. Make the supper there."

The disciples left Bethany and went into Jerusalem. They found everything just as Jesus had told them, and they made the arrangements for the Passover supper.

That evening Jesus arrived at the house with the twelve men who were his closest followers. Those disciples were:

Simon, whom Jesus called Peter
Andrew, the brother of Simon Peter
James and John, brothers who were fishermen,
    like Peter and Andrew

Philip, a man from Peter and Andrew's
    hometown
Thomas
Bartholomew
Matthew, a tax collector
James, the son of Alpheus
Simon the Zealot, who was a member of an
anti-Roman rebel group
Judas, the son of James
Judas Iscariot, the traitor
When all twelve disciples were seated at the

table, Jesus stood up and laid down his robe. He picked up a towel and tied it around his waist so he looked like a servant. Then he poured water into a basin and began to wash the disciples' feet. He dried them with the towel.

When he came to Peter, Peter said, "Are you going to wash my feet, Lord?"

Jesus answered, "What I'm doing now you don't understand, but later you'll understand."

Peter didn't want Jesus to act like a servant. "You'll never wash my feet!" he said.

Jesus answered, "If I don't wash you, you can't share my life."

"Then, Lord," said Peter, "not just my feet! Wash my hands and face also!"

Jesus said, "Anyone who has taken a bath doesn't need to be washed, except for his feet. He's clean all over. Now you men are clean—but not all of you."

He said this because he knew who was going to betray him.

"Do you understand what I've done for you?" he asked. "You call me Teacher and Lord—and that's good, because I am your Lord and Teacher. Now, then, if the Lord and Master washes your feet, you must wash each other's feet. I'm doing this as an example for you. You must do exactly as I have done.

"Remember, no servant is greater than his lord, and no messenger is greater than the one who sends him. If you understand this, you'll find happiness by doing it."

The disciples had trouble with this teaching because they were always arguing about which of them was the most important. They didn't want to be servants. They wanted to be great.

10

The Last Supper

Matthew 26; Mark 14; Luke 22; John 13

I'VE been looking forward to eating this Passover with you," Jesus told the twelve disciples. "I've wanted with all my heart to do it before I suffer, because I won't eat it again until it's given its full meaning in the kingdom of God."

While they were eating the roast lamb and the flat bread, Jesus said to them, "I tell you truly, one of you will betray me."

The disciples looked at one another. They wondered which of them he was talking about.

"Surely, Lord," they each said, "it isn't I!" They were all upset.

Jesus answered, "The Son of Man is going the way he must, as the Scripture says. But how terrible it will be for the man who betrays him! It would be better for that man if he had never been born!"

Then Peter nodded to John, who was sitting close to Jesus, and John asked, "Who is it, Lord?"

"It's one of the twelve," answered Jesus. "As Scripture says:

> 'The man who eats my bread
> has rebelled against me.'"

Then Jesus dipped a piece of bread into a bowl of sauce and handed it to Judas. The moment Judas took the bread, Satan entered him.

"What you're going to do, do quickly," said Jesus.

None of the others at the table understood why Jesus said that. Since Judas was their treasurer, some of them thought Jesus was telling him to buy what they needed for Passover. Others thought he was telling him to give something to the poor.

After he took the bread, Judas went outside. It was night.

Then Jesus said, "Now the glory of the Son of Man is coming, and the glory of God is going to show through him!"

He took a cup and gave thanks to God.

"Take this," he said, "and share it among yourselves. From now on, I won't drink the fruit of the vine until the kingdom of God comes."

While they were still eating supper, Jesus took some bread. When he had given thanks, he broke it and gave it to his disciples.

"Take and eat this," he said. "This is my body, given for you. Do this in remembrance of me."

In the same way, after supper, he took the cup of wine. And when he had given thanks, he gave it to them and said, "Drink this, all of you. This is my blood of the new covenant, which is being shed for many, for the forgiveness of sins."

After he had spoken these words, Jesus said to his disciples, "O my children! We have just a short time left together! You'll miss me, but where I'm going, you can't come."

"Lord," asked Peter, "Where are you going?"

Jesus answered, "Where I'm going, you can't follow now, but you'll follow me later."

"Why not?" asked Peter. "Why can't I follow you now? I'm ready to go anywhere with you—even to prison!"

"Peter! Peter!" said Jesus. "Watch out! Satan is going to test all of you. But I have prayed for you, Peter. I've prayed that your faith won't fail. When you have recovered, you must strengthen your brothers."

Then he said to all of them, "This very night all of you will lose faith. For Scripture says:

> 'I will strike the shepherd,
> and his sheep will be scattered.'

"But after I have risen, I will go ahead of you into Galilee."

Peter protested, "Everyone else may lose their faith, but I never will!"

"I tell you, Peter," said Jesus, "today—indeed, this very night, before the rooster crows—you will say three times you don't know me."

"Never!" said Peter. "I'll never deny you, even if I have to die with you!"

All the other disciples said the same thing.

11

The Way, the Truth, and the Life

John 14—15

DON'T worry," Jesus said to the disciples. "As you trust God, trust me. There are many rooms in my Father's house. I'm going now to prepare a place for you. After I've gone, I'll come back to take you with me. As for where I'm going—you know the way."

"Lord," said Thomas, "we don't know where you're going. How do you expect us to know the way?"

Jesus answered, "I am the way, the truth, and the life. No one can come to the Father except through me. If you really know me, you also know my Father."

"Lord," said Philip, "show us the Father! Then we'll be satisfied!"

"Philip," said Jesus, "we've been together for a long time. Don't you know me yet? Whoever has seen me has seen the Father. So how can you ask me to show you the Father?"

Then he said to all of them, "I'll ask the Father, and he'll send you another helper to be with you until the end of time. This is the Spirit of truth.

"I won't leave you alone, but I'll return. In just a little while the world won't see me anymore, but you'll see me. For I have life, and you will have life, too."

"Lord," said Judas, son of James, "what are you talking about? What does all this mean?"

Jesus answered, "Whoever loves me will obey my commandments. Then the Father will love him, and we'll come to him and live in him.

"After I leave, the Father will send the Holy Spirit to be your teacher. The Holy Spirit will remind you of everything I have taught you.

"I leave you my peace. My peace I give to you.

"Don't worry. Don't be afraid. You heard me say I'm going away and I'll return. I tell you now, before it happens, so that when it happens, you'll believe.

"I am the vine, the true vine. My Father is the gardener. He prunes the vine by cutting off every branch that doesn't produce fruit. He trims the

fruitful branches, so they can produce even more fruit. You've already been trimmed by my teaching.

"If you stay in me, I'll stay in you. A branch can't produce fruit all by itself. It has to stay on the vine. You can't produce fruit without staying in me.

"I am the vine. You are the branches. Whoever shares my life and stays in me will produce fruit.

"If you're cut off from me, you can't produce anything. You'll be like a branch that's broken off and thrown away, a dry stick that's thrown on the fire.

"But if you stay in me, whatever you ask for will be done. My Father will be glorified because of the fruit you produce.

"I have loved you as the Father has loved me. If you keep my commandments, you stay in my love as I stay in the Father's love.

"I tell you these things so you can share my joy and your joy may be complete.

This is my commandment: *Love one another as I have loved you.* Nobody can show greater love than this—to lay down his life for the ones he loves. You are the ones I love when you do as I command you.

"I don't call you servants any more, because a servant doesn't know what his master is doing. Instead, I call you my friends, for I have told you everything I've heard from my Father.

"You didn't choose me. I chose you. I send you to produce fruit that will last.

"If the world hates you, remember, it hated me first. It hates you because you don't belong to the world.

"A servant isn't greater than his master. If they persecute me, they'll certainly persecute you. Anyone who hates me hates the Father. They've seen my works and heard my teaching, but they hate me because they don't know my Father.

"When the Helper comes—the Spirit of truth whom I will send from the Father—when he comes, he will speak plainly about me."

12

Jesus Prays for His Disciples

John 16—17

WHAT does Jesus mean?" asked the disciples.

"We don't understand what he's talking about!" they said to each other.

Jesus explained, "I'm telling you that I'll soon go away. It's for your own good, for then the Holy Spirit will come and guide you.

"You'll cry when I leave, but then your sorrow will turn to joy. You'll be like a woman having a baby. When she's in labor, she suffers. But after the baby's born, she forgets the pain because of her joy that a child has been born into the world.

"You're in pain now because I'm leaving, but I'll see you again. Then your hearts will be full of joy. It will be a joy that no one can take away from you.

"I tell you the truth. Whatever you ask from the Father in my name, he will give to you. Ask and you will receive, and your joy will be overflowing.

"The Father loves you because you love me, because you believe that I come from God. I came from the Father into the world. Now I'm leaving the world and going to the Father."

"Yes," said the disciples, "now we understand. We see that you know everything. We believe that you come from God!"

"Now do you believe?" said Jesus. "The time is coming when you'll be scattered. Each of you will go his own way and leave me all alone. Yet I'm never alone, because the Father is with me.

"I've told you this so you'll find peace in me. In the world, you'll have suffering, but be brave. I have conquered the world!"

Then Jesus looked up to heaven and said this prayer:

"Father, the time has come. Glorify your Son that the Son may give glory to you. You gave him authority over all humanity, so that he may give eternal life to everyone you give him. This is eternal life: to know you, the one true God, and Jesus Christ, whom you sent.

"Father! I've made you known to the ones you gave me. Now they understand that everything you've given me comes from you. They accepted the teaching I gave them, and they believe that you sent me. I pray for them now, because they are yours. I'm no longer in the world, but they are in the world.

"Holy Father! Keep them in your name, so they may be one, as you and I are one. I don't ask you to take them out of the world, but I ask you to protect them from the evil one. Make them holy by the truth, for your word is truth. I don't pray just for them, but I also pray for the people who will believe in me through their message. I pray that they all may be one.

"Father! May they be one as you and I are one,

so the world will believe that you sent me. I gave them the same glory you gave me, so they may be one.

"Father! You have given them to me, and I want them to be with me, so they may see my glory, the glory you gave me. You loved me before the world was made.

"Father, good Father! The world doesn't know you. But I know you, and these people know that you sent me. I showed you to them. I'll keep on showing you to them, so the love you have for me will be in them!"

The Lamb
of God

13

Jesus Is Arrested

Matthew 26; Mark 14; Luke 22; John 18

AFTER they finished eating the Passover supper and listening to Jesus' teachings, the disciples sang some Passover hymns with him. Then they went out together into the dark streets of Jerusalem.

They left the city, crossed the Kidron Valley, and came to a place at the foot of the Mount of Olives, to a garden called Gethsemane. Jesus often prayed in the olive orchard there, and all the disciples knew the place well.

As they entered the garden, Jesus said to them,

"Pray that you won't fall into temptation." Then he told them, "Stay here while I go over there and pray."

He walked a little way from them, taking Peter, James, and John with him. Then he stopped, for he was loaded down with feelings of horror and sadness.

"My heart is so full of grief, it's ready to break," he said to Peter, James, and John. "Wait here and keep watch with me."

Then he went on by himself a little farther.

"My Father!" cried Jesus, throwing himself onto the ground. "Everything is possible for you. Take this cup of suffering away from me!" Then he prayed, "Yet, not what I want, but what you want."

He went back to the place where he had left Peter, James, and John. They were asleep.

"Peter!" said Jesus. "Are you asleep? Didn't you have enough strength to stay awake for even an hour?"

Then he said to the three of them, "Stay on guard, all of you. Pray that you won't be put to the test. Your spirits are eager, but human nature is weak."

He left them a second time, and again he prayed, "My Father! If this cup can't pass by without my drinking it, then your will be done!"

He returned to the disciples. Again he found them sleeping. They couldn't keep their eyes open.

For a third time he left them and went to pray. He prayed the same prayer.

Then an angel from heaven appeared and strengthened him. He was in agony, and he prayed even harder. His sweat fell to the ground like great drops of blood.

Then he stood up and walked back to the disciples.

"Are you still sleeping?" he asked. "Still taking your rest? Enough. The time has come. Now the Son of Man is handed over to sinners. Get up! Let's go. See, my betrayer is near!"

While Jesus was still speaking, Judas Iscariot appeared. He came into the garden with a force of Roman soldiers and temple police sent by the chief priests, scribes, and elders. They were carrying swords and clubs and lighted torches.

Judas had arranged to give a signal to the men with him, so they would know which one was Jesus.

"The man you want is the one I kiss," Judas had told them. "Arrest him and take him away under guard."

When Judas arrived, he went up to Jesus and said, "Peace, Teacher!" and kissed him.

"Judas," said Jesus, "are you betraying the Son of Man with a kiss?"

Then he said to the soldiers and police, "Well, do what you're here for."

They grabbed Jesus. In the confusion Peter took out his sword and attacked the servant of

the high priest, a man named Malchus, and cut off his right ear.

"Put your sword away," said Jesus. "I must go through this suffering. I must drink the cup the Father has given me." Then he touched the man's ear and healed him.

"Everyone who takes up the sword will die by the sword," he told the disciples. "Don't you realize that I could call on my Father, and he would send fifty thousand angels to defend me? But then how could the Scripture be fulfilled? These things must happen."

Then he spoke to the men who had come for him. "Am I a bandit, that you have come to capture me with swords and clubs? Day after day I sat among you teaching in the temple, and you didn't arrest me. But this is your hour. This is the reign of darkness."

Then they arrested him and took him away under guard, and the disciples ran away. They scattered in every direction, like sheep.

14

Jesus Is Condemned and Denied

Matthew 26—27; Mark 14—15; Luke 22; John 18

JESUS was taken out of the garden with his hands tied together. The Roman soldiers and the temple police took him to Annas, the father-in-law of the high priest.

Peter and another disciple followed them. This other disciple was known to the high priest. He went with Jesus into the high priest's palace, while Peter stayed outside at the gate.

The other disciple went out and spoke to the woman who was guarding the door. Then he brought Peter into the courtyard of the palace.

Since it was cold, the servants and the guards had lit a charcoal fire and they were standing around it, warming themselves. Peter went and stood with them, waiting to see how it would all end.

Inside the high priest's palace, Annas and the other chief priests were questioning Jesus about his disciples and his teaching.

"I've spoken openly for all the world to hear," Jesus told them. "I've always taught in the synagogues and the temple. I've said nothing in secret. Why do you question me? Why don't you question the people who heard my teaching? They know what I said."

When he said this, one of the officers standing there gave him a slap in the face. "Is that any way to answer the high priest?" he said.

Jesus answered, "If I've said anything wrong, show me. But if what I've said is true, why do you hit me?"

Then Annas sent Jesus with his hands still tied to Caiaphas, the high priest.

The chief priests met with Caiaphas to find evidence to use against Jesus. They didn't care if people lied, because they were looking for an excuse to condemn Jesus to death.

Many witnesses came forward and lied about Jesus, but their stories weren't the same. According to the law, the story of two witnesses had to agree before the court could sentence someone to death.

Finally two liars stood up and spoke against him. They testified, "We heard this man say, 'I will tear down the temple made with hands and build another one not made with hands.'" But even their stories didn't match.

"Well," said Caiaphas as he stood up and walked to the middle of the hall, "do you have an answer to that testimony?" He stared at Jesus. "What do you say about the evidence these men have given against you?"

Jesus was silent. He didn't answer the men who were accusing him.

Then Caiaphas said, "I put you under oath, by the living God! Tell us, are you the Messiah?"

"The words are yours," said Jesus. "The time is coming when you'll see the Son of Man sitting at the right hand of God Almighty and coming with the clouds of heaven."

"So you're the Son of God?" they asked.

"I am," he answered.

"What do we need any more witnesses for?" cried Caiaphas. "You've heard it from his own lips. He's speaking blasphemy!"

Then Caiaphas tore his robe as a sign that Jesus had insulted God, that he had claimed to be God.

"What's your verdict?" Caiaphas asked the priests. "What have you decided?"

"He must die!" they answered.

Then some of the guards went up to Jesus and spit at him and beat him with their fists. They

blindfolded him and mocked him, saying, "Prophesy, you messiah! Tell us who hit you!"

This happened in the middle of the night. When morning came, the chief priests met with the scribes and elders, the whole group of seventy men that made up the ruling council of the Jews.

After meeting to plan Jesus' death, the members of the council had Jesus put in chains. The soldiers led him away to be handed over to the Roman governor, a man named Pontius Pilate.

While this was going on upstairs, Peter was downstairs in the courtyard of the high priest's palace.

One of the high priest's servants went up to

him. When she saw him warming himself by the fire, she said, "Weren't you with Jesus of Nazareth?"

"Woman," answered Peter, "I don't know him."

Then one of the temple guards said, "You must be a disciple of that man. I can tell by your accent that you're from Galilee."

"I don't know what you're talking about," said Peter. "I don't know him!"

A little while later a relative of Malchus, the man whose ear Peter had cut off, came up to him and said, "Didn't I see you with that fellow in the garden?"

"No," said Peter. "I swear I don't know him!"

While he was still speaking, a rooster began to crow. Peter looked up and saw Jesus being taken away in chains. Peter remembered what Jesus had said earlier that evening: "Before the rooster crows, you will say three times you don't know me."

Peter went outside and cried.

15

The King of the Jews

Matthew 27; Mark 15; Luke 23; John 19; Acts 1

WHEN Judas Iscariot found out that Jesus had been sentenced to death, he changed his mind and was sorry for what he had done. He took the thirty pieces of silver and gave them back to the chief priests and the elders.

"I have sinned," he said. "I have betrayed an innocent man."

"What do we care?" they said. "That's your problem."

Judas threw the coins down in the temple and left. Then he went out and hanged himself.

The chief priests picked up the silver pieces and said, "It's against the law to put this into the temple treasury. It's blood money."

They talked it over and decided to use the money to buy the potter's field as a cemetery for foreigners. That is why the field became known as the Field of Blood.

In this way the words of Scripture came true:

"They took thirty pieces of silver,
    the price they set on the Precious One.
"They used the money to buy the potter's field,
    as the Lord commanded."

The council took Jesus from the high priest's palace to the palace of the Roman governor. They didn't go inside the governor's palace, because they had rules against entering the house of a non-Jew, especially at Passover time. These religious leaders were very careful to keep themselves pure in the eyes of God.

Pilate came out to meet the high priest and the seventy members of the council. "What charges are you bringing against this man?" he asked.

"This fellow is a criminal," they answered, "or we wouldn't be handing him over to you. We found him stirring up our people and encouraging them to rebel. He spoke against paying taxes to Caesar. He even claimed to be an anointed king, a christ."

"Take him yourselves," said Pilate. "Put him

on trial according to your own law."

"We can't," they reminded Pilate. "We're not allowed to carry out the death penalty. Only you Romans can execute criminals."

Pilate went back inside his palace and called Jesus to him so he could question him.

"Are you the king of the Jews?" he asked.

Jesus said, "Do you ask this on your own, or have other people been telling you about me?"

"Surely," said Pilate, "you don't think I'm a Jew! Your own people and the chief priests have handed you over to me. What have you done?"

Jesus answered, "My kingdom doesn't belong to this world. If my kingdom belonged to this world, my subjects would be fighting to save me. But my kingdom isn't like other kingdoms."

"So you're a king?" said Pilate.

"The words are yours," said Jesus. "The reason I've been born and have come into the world is to witness to the truth. Everyone who belongs to the truth listens to my voice."

"Truth?" asked Pilate. "What is truth?"

Then Pilate went to the chief priests and said, "I find no reason to condemn this man to death."

But they insisted. "He's been stirring up the people with his teaching," they said, "beginning in Galilee and all the way down here—all over Judea."

"Oh?" said Pilate. "Is this man a Galilean?"

When Pilate found out that Jesus came from Galilee, he sent him to Herod Antipas, ruler of Galilee. Herod Antipas, a son of King Herod the Great, was in Jerusalem for the Passover

Herod was delighted to see Jesus. He had wanted to meet him for a long time, because he had heard so much about him. He was hoping to see Jesus work a miracle.

Herod asked him a lot of questions, but Jesus wouldn't answer. All this time the chief priests and scribes stood by, violently accusing him.

Finally, Herod sent him away, saying that he was worthless. Before Jesus left, Herod's soldiers mocked him. Then they took him back to Pilate.

Although Herod and Pilate had been enemies, that day they became friends.

16

The Crown of Thorns

Matthew 27; Mark 15; Luke 23

PILATE wasn't co-operating with the Jewish leaders. The council needed his permission to put Jesus to death. But Pilate didn't want to have him killed.

"You have accused this man of stirring up a rebellion," Pilate said to the chief priests and elders. "I've questioned him, and I don't find him guilty of any crime. Neither does Herod, for he has sent the man back to me. Obviously, Jesus hasn't done anything to deserve the death penalty, despite all the things you've accused him of. I'll have him punished and let him go."

He took Jesus and turned him over to his soldiers to be beaten. They twisted some thorns into a crown and put it on his head. Then they put a robe of royal purple on him and placed a stick in his right hand.

"All hail!" cried the soldiers, mocking him. "King of the Jews!" They went up to him and bowed, and then they spit on him. They slapped his face and took the stick and beat him over the head with it.

When the soldiers were finished, Pilate said, "Look, I'm going to take him out to show them that I find no case against him."

Jesus went out wearing the crown of thorns and the purple robe.

"Look!" said Pilate. "See the man!"

The priests had gathered a crowd in front of Pilate's palace, and the crowd shouted, "Not this man. We want Barabbas!"

Barabbas was a bandit who was in prison for causing riot and murder. It was the custom for the Roman governor to set one prisoner free at Passover, and the chief priests had told the people to ask Pilate to free Barabbas.

Pilate asked them, "Then what should I do with this Jesus?"

"Crucify him!" they shouted. "Crucify him!"

"Take him and crucify him yourselves," said Pilate. "I find no case against him."

He knew that they wanted him to have Jesus

killed because they were jealous.

"We have our own law," said the priests. "According to our law, he must die because he pretended to be the Son of God."

When he heard this, Pilate was more afraid than ever. He went back into the palace and sat down on the judge's bench. While he was sitting there, he received a message from his wife.

"Have nothing to do with that innocent man," she said. "I've been upset all day because of a dream I had about him last night."

Then Pilate turned to Jesus and said, "Where do you come from?"

Jesus wouldn't answer.

"Do you refuse to speak to me?" asked Pilate. "Don't you realize that I have the power to set you free—and the power to crucify you?"

Jesus answered, "You have no power at all against me—except what has been given to you from above."

After this, Pilate was eager to set Jesus free.

"If you set him free," said the priests, "you're no friend of Caesar. Anyone who pretends to be a king is rebelling against Caesar."

Pilate realized that the priests would accuse him of being a traitor to Caesar if he didn't do what they wanted. He took Jesus outside again.

"Look!" he said. "Here is your king."

"Take him away," they shouted. "Crucify him!"

"What?" said Pilate. "Do you want me to crucify your king?"

"We have no king except Caesar," they answered.

Pilate realized that he couldn't change their minds, and he was afraid that a riot would break out. So he took a bowl of water and washed his hands right there in front of them.

"I'm innocent of condemning an innocent man to death," he said as he washed his hands. "It's your responsibility."

"That's all right with us!" they cried.

Then Pilate handed Jesus over to them to be crucified.

The Lamb of God

Matthew 27; Mark 15; Luke 23; John 19

FOUR soldiers took Jesus out of the city. They made him carry his own cross. A large crowd followed him, including many crying women.

"Daughters of Jerusalem," he said, turning to them. "Don't cry for me. Instead, cry for yourselves and your children, for the time is coming when Jerusalem will be destroyed, and all its people will suffer."

On the way to the place where Jesus was to be executed, they met a man from Cyrene. This man was a North African named Simon who was on his way to the city. The soldiers forced him to carry Jesus' cross.

They arrived at a place outside the city called Golgotha, which means "the hill of the skull." (In Latin it was called Calvary.)

At Golgotha the soldiers set up three crosses. They nailed Jesus to the middle cross and nailed robbers on the other two crosses. It was nine o'clock in the morning.

As he was being crucified, Jesus prayed, "Father, forgive them, for they don't know what they're doing."

After they finished nailing Jesus to the cross, the soldiers took his clothes and divided them into four parts. Since his tunic was woven in one piece, one of the soldiers said, "Instead of tearing it up into four pieces, let's throw dice and see who wins it."

In this way the words of Scripture came true:

> "They divided up my clothes among them;
> they rolled dice for my clothing."

That was exactly what the soldiers did. Then they sat down and kept guard over him.

Pilate had a notice written and placed above the cross. It stated the charge against him: JESUS OF NAZARETH, THE KING OF THE JEWS.

Many people read the notice, for the place

where Jesus was crucified was near the city and the writing was in three languages—Hebrew, Latin, and Greek.

When the priests saw the notice, they were so annoyed, they asked Pilate to change the writing.

"Don't leave it written 'The King of the Jews,'" they complained. "Instead, write, 'This man said he was the King of the Jews.'"

Pilate answered, "What I have written, I have written."

People who were passing by and people who were standing around to watch the crucifixion shook their heads and insulted Jesus.

"Aha!" they said. "You were going to pull down

the temple and rebuild it in three days! Now save yourself and come down from the cross!"

The chief priests and the scribes went out to Calvary to mock him. "He saved others," they said to each other. "But he can't save himself. Let the 'Messiah,' 'the king of Israel,' come down from the cross now."

"He trusts God. Well, let's see if God rescues him!"

"He said he was the Son of God. If we see God rescue him, then we'll believe in him."

The Roman soldiers mocked him, too. "If you're really the king of the Jews," they said, "save yourself."

Even one of the criminals who was dying on the cross next to Jesus began to insult him.

"Aren't you the Messiah?" he asked. "Then save yourself—and us, too!"

The second robber scolded the first one. "Don't you fear God?" he warned. "After all, you received the same sentence this man did. For us it's fair, for we deserve to pay for our crimes. But this man has done nothing wrong."

Then he said to Jesus, "Remember me when you come into your kingdom."

"I promise you," said Jesus, "today you'll be with me in paradise."

Some of Jesus' friends were at Calvary, watching everything from a distance. Standing near the cross were his mother, his mother's sister, Mary the wife of Clopas, and Mary Magdalene.

When Jesus saw his mother there with John, his beloved disciple, he said to her, "Woman, here is your son." And he said to John, "Here is your mother."

From that time on, John took care of Jesus' mother in his home.

At noon darkness came over the whole land, and it lasted for three hours.

At about three o'clock Jesus spoke again. To fulfill the Scripture perfectly, he said, "I am thirsty."

The soldiers soaked a sponge in some wine and lifted it up to his lips on a hyssop stick. (When the Israelites were slaves in Egypt, the blood of the sacrificed lamb was spread on the doorposts with hyssop sticks.)

Before he tasted the wine, Jesus cried out in a loud voice, "My God! My God! Why have you left me?"

Then he said, "It is finished," and with a loud cry, he handed his spirit over to his Father.

As he died, the curtain in the holy place inside the temple was torn in two, from top to bottom. At the same time, the earth shook, rocks split apart, and graves were opened.

A Roman officer standing in front of the cross said, "Truly, this man was the Son of God!"

18

In the Tomb

Matthew 27; Mark 15; Luke 23; John 19

CRUCIFIXION was a painful way to die. Usually the criminals died slowly, hanging on their crosses for several days. But this was Passover week. It was also the day before the Sabbath. The Jewish leaders didn't want the bodies left out after sundown, so they asked Pilate to hurry up the executions by having the legs broken and the bodies taken away.

The soldiers then broke the legs of the robbers who were crucified on each side of Jesus. When they came to Jesus' cross, they saw that he was already dead, so they didn't break his legs. Instead, one of the soldiers pierced Jesus' side with a spear. Immediately, blood and water flowed from his side.

These things happened to fulfill the Scriptures:

"Not one of his bones will be broken.
They will look on the one whom they have pierced."

It was nearly sunset when Joseph of Arimathea arrived. Joseph was a rich man and a member of the council. He hadn't agreed with their decision to condemn Jesus to death, for he was a secret follower of Jesus.

Now Joseph went boldly to Pilate and asked him for Jesus' body. Pilate was surprised to hear that Jesus was already dead, and he called for the officer in charge to ask if it was really true. After he heard the officer's report, Pilate gave Joseph permission to take the body.

Joseph went to the cross with Nicodemus, another member of the council who knew Jesus. Joseph took a linen sheet to wrap around the body, and Nicodemus took a hundred pounds of spices to anoint it.

When they reached the cross, they took down the body and wrapped it with the spices in the linen shroud. Since it was almost evening, and the beginning of the Sabbath, they took the body to a tomb to bury it.

Near Calvary was a garden, and in the garden

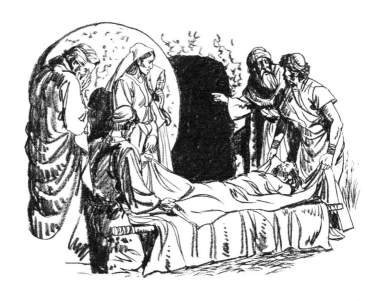

was a tomb that belonged to Joseph. It had just been dug out of solid rock and had never been used. Joseph and Nicodemus put Jesus' body in the tomb. Then they rolled a large stone across the entrance.

The women who had come from Galilee with Jesus had followed Joseph and Nicodemus to the tomb. They watched carefully to see how the body was laid. Then they went away to prepare ointments to bring after the Sabbath.

The sun went down and it was the Sabbath day, the Jewish day of rest.

While Jesus' friends rested, as the Sabbath law required, the chief priests and the Pharisees went to Pilate with a request.

"Your excellency!" they said. "We remember that while he was still alive, that imposter said he would be raised to life in three days. So we're making this request: give orders to have the tomb carefully guarded for the next three days. We're afraid that his disciples may come and steal the body and then tell the people that he has risen from the dead. If they do, this last piece of fraud will be worse than the first!"

"You can have your guard," said Pilate. "Go back and make the tomb as secure as you can."

They went and set soldiers on guard at the tomb. They even put seals on the stone, to make sure that no one could come and steal the body.

God Shows
His Glory

19

The Empty Tomb

Matthew 28; Mark 16; Luke 24; John 20

EARLY on the first day of the week, the day after the Sabbath, some of the women went to visit the tomb. They were bringing spices to anoint Jesus' body, according to the Jewish custom. It was still dark when they started out.

"Who will roll the stone away?" they asked each other on the way. They remembered that the entrance of the tomb was covered by a huge stone.

Just as the sun was rising, they reached the tomb. The stone had been rolled away.

They went inside, and there, sitting on the right, they saw a young man in a white robe. They were terrified.

"Don't be afraid," he said. "You're looking for Jesus of Nazareth, who was crucified. He isn't here, for he has risen. See the place where they laid him. Now go and tell his disciples that he's going ahead of them to Galilee, where they will see him, as he promised."

The women left the tomb and ran to tell the disciples what the angel had said. They were trembling with fear.

When the disciples heard the women's story, they didn't believe it. "Nonsense!" they scoffed.

Still, Peter and John decided to go and see for

themselves. They ran off, side by side. John passed Peter and reached the tomb first. He bent down to look in and saw the linen wrappings lying there, but he didn't go in.

Peter came running up behind John. He went straight into the tomb and saw the linen cloths lying there, and the piece of cloth that had covered the head. It was with the linen cloth, but it was folded up in a place by itself.

John went in and saw this, and he believed.

After John and Peter left the garden tomb, Mary Magdalene came and stood outside, crying. She stooped down to look inside. She saw two angels in white sitting where the body had been, one at the head and one at the foot.

"Woman," said the angels, "why are you crying?"

"Because they've taken my Master away," she answered them. "I don't know where they've put him."

"Don't be afraid," said the angel.

Mary turned and saw Jesus standing there, but she didn't recognize him.

"Woman," he said, "why are you crying? Whom are you looking for?"

She thought he was the gardener, so she said, "Sir, if you're the one who took him away, tell me where you've put him, and I'll go get him."

Jesus said, "Mary!"

She turned to him and said, "Teacher!"

"Peace be with you," he said.

She fell down in front of him, worshiping him, and took hold of his feet.

"Don't cling to me," he told her, "for I haven't gone up to the Father yet. Go and tell my brothers that I'm going up to my Father and your Father, to my God and your God."

Mary went back to the disciples and announced, "I have seen the Lord!" She told them what he had said to her.

Meanwhile, the soldiers who had been guarding the tomb went back to Jerusalem and told the chief priests about the empty tomb.

The chief priests met with the elders, and after they talked it over together, they decided to give a large bribe to the soldiers.

They said to them, "Tell the people that Jesus' disciples came during the night and stole his body while you were sleeping. If Pilate hears about it, we'll tell him you're innocent. Don't worry. We'll make sure you don't get into trouble."

The soldiers took the money and spread the story that the disciples had stolen Jesus' body.

20

Jesus Appears to His Disciples

Mark 16; Luke 24

THAT same day, the first day of the week, two of Jesus' followers were going to a village named Emmaus, about seven miles from Jerusalem. On their way into the country, they talked to each other about all the things that had been happening.

As they were talking, Jesus himself came up and began to walk along with them, but their eyes were kept from recognizing him.

"What's all this you're talking about as you walk along?" he asked them.

They stopped for a moment. Their faces were sad and gloomy. Then one of the men, Cleopas, said to him, "You must be the only visitor to Jerusalem who doesn't know the things that have happened there the past few days."

"What things?" he asked.

"The things that happened to Jesus of Nazareth," they answered. "He was a great prophet in the sight of God and all the people. He was considered to be powerful in everything he said and did.

"Haven't you heard how our chief priests and elders handed him over to be condemned? He was sentenced to death and crucified. We were hoping that he would be the one to set Israel free!"

"That's not all!" said the other disciple. "It's

been three days since all this happened. Yet some of the women from our group have really shocked us. They went to the tomb early this morning, and when they didn't find the body, they came back to tell us they had seen a vision of angels who told them Jesus is alive. Some of our friends also went to the tomb, and they found everything exactly as the women had said. But they didn't see Jesus."

"Foolish people!" said Jesus. "So slow to put your trust in everything the prophets said! Wasn't the Messiah bound to suffer all this before entering into his glory?"

Then, beginning with the books of Moses and the writings of all the prophets, he explained to them the passages of Scripture that were about himself.

As they came near the village of Emmaus, Jesus acted as though he planned to go on.

"Stay here with us," they urged him. "It's almost evening and getting dark."

He went into the village to stay with them. While he was with them at supper, he took bread and said a blessing. As he broke it and gave it to them, their eyes were opened, and they recognized him. Then he vanished from their sight.

They turned to each other and said, "Didn't our hearts burn within us as he talked to us on the way and explained the Scripture to us?"

Even though it was late, they immediately got

up and went back to Jerusalem. There they found the eleven leading disciples gathered together with the others.

"It's really true!" they were saying. "The Lord has risen! He has appeared to Peter!"

Then the two disciples who had gone to Emmaus explained what had happened to them on the way. They told how Jesus had become known to them in the breaking of the bread.

"Blessed Are Those Who Believe"

Luke 24; John 20

THE disciples were in a room with the doors shut, because they were afraid that the religious leaders would come for them. They were still talking about the things they had seen and heard when suddenly Jesus came and stood in front of them.

"Peace be with you," he said.

The disciples stepped back in terror. They thought he was a ghost.

"Why are you upset?" he asked. "Why do these questions rise in your minds?"

He showed them his wounds. "Look at my hands and feet," he said. "It is I myself! Touch. Look. Ghosts don't have flesh and bones like this!"

The disciples were so full of joy, they couldn't believe it. They just stood there, completely amazed.

"Do you have anything to eat?" Jesus asked them.

They gave him some cooked fish, and he took it and ate it in front of them.

"Here and now," he said, "everything I taught you while I was with you is coming true. Everything written about me in the Law and the Prophets and the Psalms is being fulfilled."

Then he opened their minds so they could understand the Scriptures.

"This is what the Scriptures say," he told them. "The Messiah must suffer and rise from the dead on the third day. In his name the message about turning to God and God's forgiveness of sins must be preached to all nations, beginning in Jerusalem.

"You are witnesses to what has happened. I give you the gift my Father has promised. Peace be with you. As the Father has sent me, so I send you."

Then he breathed on them and said, "Receive the Holy Spirit. If you forgive people's sins, they will be forgiven. If you don't forgive them, they will not be forgiven. Now stay in Jerusalem until

you have been given power from heaven."

One of the disciples, Thomas, was absent when Jesus came. Later, when Jesus was gone and Thomas had arrived, they kept telling him they had seen the Lord.

"I can't believe it," said Thomas. "Unless I see the mark of the nails on his hands and put my fingers into the place the nails made and my hand into his side, I won't believe it!"

A week later the disciples were in the house again. This time Thomas was with them. The doors were locked.

Then Jesus came and stood in front of them.

"Peace be with you," he said to them. Then he said to Thomas, "Reach out your finger and examine my hands. Reach out your hand and put it in my side. Don't keep doubting, but become a believer!"

Thomas answered, "My Lord and my God!"

Jesus said to him, "You believe because you can see me. Blessed are those who have not seen and yet believe."

"Feed My Lambs"

John 21

I'M GOING fishing," said Peter.

"We'll go with you," said the other disciples. They were beside the Sea of Galilee.

Peter, Thomas, Nathanael, James, John, and two other disciples went out and got into a fishing boat. That night they didn't catch anything.

In the morning, right after the sun came up, Jesus stood on the shore. None of the disciples realized who he was.

"Hey, boys!" he called out. "Have you caught anything to eat?"

"No," they answered.

He said, "Throw the net out to the right side of the boat, and you'll find something."

They threw out the net, and it filled with so many fish, they couldn't pull it in.

Then John said to Peter, "It's the Lord!"

When he heard it was the Lord, Peter pulled on his cloak and jumped into the lake.

The other disciples went to Jesus in the boat, towing the net of fish behind them. They were only about a hundred yards from shore. They landed and saw a charcoal fire and some bread. A fish was cooking on the fire.

"Bring some of the fish you caught just now," said Jesus.

Peter went back to the boat and dragged the net to the shore. It was full of large fish—one hundred and fifty-three of them. Despite the large catch, the net didn't tear.

"Come and eat breakfast!" said Jesus.

None of the disciples dared to ask him who he was. They realized it was the Lord.

Jesus came over and took the bread and gave it to them, and also the fish.

When they had finished eating, he said to Peter, "Peter, do you love me more than these?"

"Yes, Lord," he answered. "You know I love you."

"Then feed my lambs," said Jesus.

Again he asked, "Peter, do you love me?"

"Yes, Lord," said Peter. "You know I love you."

"Then look after my sheep," he said.

A third time Jesus asked, "Peter, do you love me?"

Peter was hurt that Jesus asked him a third time if he loved him. "Lord," he said, "you know everything. You know I love you."

"Feed my lambs," said Jesus. Then he added, "I tell you the truth. When you were a young man, you fastened your own belt and walked wherever you pleased. But when you grow old, you'll stretch out your hands and someone else will fasten a belt around you and take you where you don't want to go."

He was talking about the kind of death Peter would suffer, and how it would bring glory to God.

Then he said, "Follow me," and Peter turned and saw John behind them.

"What about him, Lord?" he asked.

Jesus answered, "If I want him to stay until I come, what does that matter to you? Follow me!"

Because Jesus said this about John, some of the disciples thought he meant that John wouldn't die, though this wasn't what he said.

23

Jesus Goes Up to Heaven

Matthew 28; Mark 16; Luke 24

THE eleven disciples went to a mountain in Galilee where Jesus had arranged to meet them. When they saw him, they fell down and worshiped him, although some doubted.

Jesus came up to them and spoke to them, telling them to go to the world as missionaries, with the power he would give them.

"I have been given all power in heaven and earth," he said. "Go into every part of the world and preach the good news of God's rule. Make disciples from every nation. Baptize them in the

name of the Father and the Son and the Holy
Spirit. Teach them to obey all the commandments I have given to you."

He lifted his hands and blessed them. "Remember," he said. "I am with you always, until
the end of time!"

Then, as they watched, Jesus was taken up to
heaven. As he left them, they worshiped him.

Then the disciples went back to Jerusalem.
Their hearts were filled with great joy, just as
Jesus had promised. They spent all their time in
the temple, giving thanks to God.

24

God Shows His Glory

John 1

IN THE beginning was the Word.
The Word was Jesus, and he was with God,
and he was God.
He was with God when the world was created.
Everything was created through him
Nothing was created without him.
Life was created in him.
That life was the light of humanity.
The light is shining in the darkness,
for the darkness could not conquer it.
He was in the world—the world that was made

through him—
   and the world did not recognize him.
He came to his own people,
   and his own people did not accept him.
But to everyone who accepted him,
   he gave the power to become
      a child of God.
The Word of God became a human being.
   He lived among us,
      full of lasting love.
We saw his glory—
   glory such as comes
      from a father to an only son.
Indeed, from his full hands
   we have all of us received
      love upon love.
The Law was God's gift through Moses.
   This lasting love came through Jesus Christ.
No one has ever seen God.
   It is God the only Son,
      who is always at the Father's side,
Who has shown us
   what God is like.

JERUSALEM AT THE TIME OF THE CRUCIFIXION

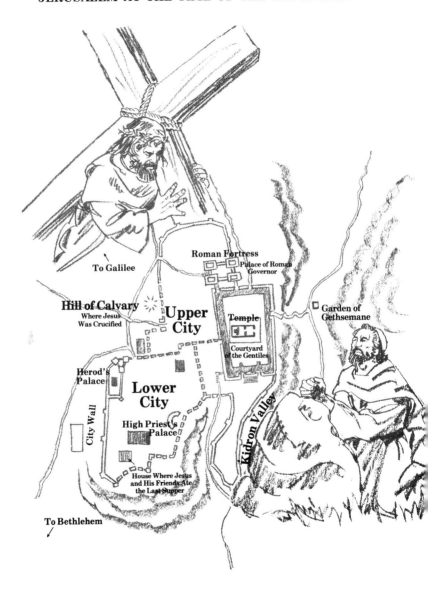

To Galilee

Roman Fortress
Palace of Roman Governor

Hill of Calvary
Where Jesus Was Crucified

Upper City

Temple

Garden of Gethsemane

Courtyard of the Gentiles

Herod's Palace

Lower City

City Wall

High Priest's Palace

Kidron Valley

House Where Jesus and His Friends Ate the Last Supper

To Bethlehem

Eve Bowers MacMaster graduated from Pennsylvania State University and George Washington University. She also studied at Harvard University and Eastern Mennonite Seminary. She has taught in the Bible department at Eastern Mennonite College and in the history department at James Madison University, both located in Harrisonburg, Virginia.

Eve visited many of the places mentioned in the Bible while she was serving as a Peace Corps volunteer in Turkey.

Eve and her husband, Richard, live at Bluffton, Ohio, with their children, Sam, Tom, and Sarah.